First Facts

The LIFE and TIMES of
George Washington
and the
American Revolution

by Marissa Kirkman

CAPSTONE PRESS
a capstone imprint

First Facts are published by Capstone Press,
1710 Roe Crest Drive, North Mankato, Minnesota 56003
www.mycapstone.com

Library of Congress Cataloging-in-Publication Data
Names: Kirkman, Marissa, author.
Title: The life and times of George Washington and the American
Revolution / by Marissa Kirkman.
Description: North Mankato, Minnesota : Capstone Press, 2017. | Series: First
    facts. Life and times | Includes bibliographical references and index. |
    Audience: 7 to 9. | Audience: K to Grade 3.
Identifiers: LCCN 2016009012 | ISBN 9781515724766 (library binding) |
ISBN 9781515724841 (pbk.) | ISBN 9781515724889 (ebook (pdf)
Subjects: LCSH: Washington, George, 1732–1799—Juvenile literature. |
    Presidents—United States—Biography—Juvenile literature. |
    Generals—United States—Biography—Juvenile literature. | United
    States—History—Revolution, 1775–1783—Juvenile literature.
Classification: LCC E312.66 .K57 2017 | DDC 973.4/1092–dc23
LC record available at http://lccn.loc.gov/2016009012

Editorial Credits

Charmaine Whitman, designer; Tracy Cummins, media researcher;
Tori Abraham, production specialist

Image Credits

Capstone Press: 5; Library of Congress: Cover Right, Cover Left, 8, 11,
15; New York Public Library/The Miriam and Ira D. Wallach Division of
Art, Prints and Photographs: 16; North Wind Picture Archives: 7, 9, 17;
Shutterstock: Apostrophe, Design Element, Susan Law Cain, 12; Wikimedia:
aoc.gov, 19, Google Cultural Institute/mQHNeuM-x3rvNw, 1, John
Trumbull, 13, nga.gov/exhibitions/2005/stuart/philadelphia.shtm, 21

Printed in the United States of America in North Mankato, Minnnesota.
009683F16

Table of Contents

The Early Colonies

Before the United States was a country, it was a group of **colonies** ruled by Great Britain. The first 13 colonies were formed along the east coast during the 1600s. Over time the colonies grew. George Washington was born in the Virginia colony in 1732. Washington and the other **colonists** followed the laws set by Great Britain.

Fact: The colonies were formed as a way to make more money. Great Britain thought there was gold and riches in the new land.

colony—an area that has been settled by people from another country

colonist—a person who lives in a colony

Lake Superior

Lake Michigan

Lake Huron

Lake Ontario

Lake Erie

(part of Massachusetts)

N.H.

New York

Hudson R.

Mass. • Boston

Conn.

R.I.

New York

Pennsylvania

Philadelphia • New Jersey

Maryland

Delaware

Virginia

Chesapeake Bay

Jamestown

Atlantic Ocean

North Carolina

South Carolina

Georgia

Charleston

☐ First Thirteen Colonies

N

0   100   200 miles

0   100   200 kilometers

5

British or American?

Some colonists were happy to follow the laws of Great Britain, while others were not. By the 1700s, many colonists felt more American than British. Many had been born in the colonies and had never been to Great Britain. These colonists did not think they should have to follow laws made by a king that was so far away. Washington was one of these colonists.

Fact: The colonies began with a few hundred people and grew to over a million by 1750.

Too Many Taxes

Many colonists questioned many of Great Britain's laws. They did not have a say in how laws were made. Colonists thought the **taxes** were unfair, so they did not pay them. King George III sent **soldiers** to America to force the colonists to follow his laws. The colonists didn't listen to the soldiers and refused to buy goods from Great Britain. Great Britain added more laws and taxes for the colonies.

tax—money that people or businesses must give to the government to pay for what the government does

8   **soldier**—a person who is in the military

King George III

Fact: The colonists had to pay high taxes on many things they used every day. They had to pay taxes on paper, sugar, and tea.

Fight for Freedom

In 1774 Washington and other colonial leaders wrote a letter to King George III. They asked for changes and a say in **government**. The king did not listen and sent more soldiers to America in April 1775. The colonists decided to fight for their **freedom**. The first **battle** of the Revolutionary War began in Lexington, Massachusetts. Colonial leaders met again and made Washington the leader of the Continental army.

---

government—the group of people who make laws, rules, and decisions for a country or state

freedom—the right to live the way you want

battle—a fight between two military groups

Fact: The colonists needed to be ready when British soldiers arrived. Paul Revere and others rode horses through the night to warn others once the British arrived.

Declaring Independence

British and American soldiers continued to fight. Many colonists wanted to be free from Great Britain and to form a new country. On July 4, 1776, colonial leaders signed the **Declaration of Independence**. It announced to Great Britain that the colonies were now the United States of America. It also **declared** war with Great Britain. Great Britain did not want to lose its colonies.

Fact: Washington did not sign the Declaration of Independence. He was leading American soldiers in the war.

the Declaration of Independence

The signing of the Declaration of Independence

Declaration of Independence—a document written by Thomas Jefferson in 1776; it declares the United States a free and independent country and says that every U.S. citizen has rights that the government should protect

declare—to make known openly or officially

Washington's Army

As leader of the Continental army, Washington trained his men to be soldiers. Unlike the British, many American soldiers had never fought in a war. At times the army did not have enough food, **supplies**, or even shoes. Washington was a strong leader. He helped his soldiers remember why they were fighting. In 1776 he led his army to beat the British in the Battle of Trenton.

Fact: The winter of 1777–1778 was very hard for Washington's army. Many soldiers died because they were hungry, sick, or cold.

supplies—materials needed to do something

Others Offer Help

For nearly eight years, Washington led his army in many battles. As the war went on, other countries offered to help the colonies. France had lost a war to the British. France's government sent soldiers and money to help the colonists. Baron von Steuben came from Prussia to help **train** the Continental army. This helped the army become stronger.

Fact: Because of von Steuben's help, fewer soldiers became sick. He made sure the soldiers kept their camps clean, which kept them from getting sick.

train—to prepare for something by learning and practicing new skills

Baron von Steuben

Washington welcomed the French soldiers who came to help the Continental army.

End of the War

Finally on October 17, 1781, the British **surrendered** to Washington at the Battle of Yorktown. Washington was a hero. The fighting soon ended in the colonies, and the war was over. British and American leaders signed a **treaty**. They agreed that the United States of America was now its own country. It was not a part of Great Britain anymore. The British soldiers finally left the colonies.

surrender—to give up in battle

treaty—a written agreement between countries or groups of people. A treaty is signed by the people's leaders.

Fact: British and American leaders signed the Treaty of Paris almost two years after the Battle of Yorktown.

President Washington

The Americans had to decide what laws to make for their country. They would also need to choose a leader. Many agreed that Washington had been a strong leader in the war. They thought he would make a great president. At first, Washington didn't want to be president. Finally he agreed and was **elected** as the first U.S. president in 1789.

Fact: There were only 11 states in the United States when Washington became president. Five more states were added while he was in office.

---

elect—to choose someone as a leader by voting

Amazing but True!

Washington knew that he had to be a strong and fair president. He knew that he would set an example for those who became president after him. Washington served as president for eight years. He then left office and returned to his Virginia home, Mount Vernon. He died there in 1799.

Glossary

battle (BA-tuhl)—a fight between two military groups

colonist (KAH-luh-nist)—a person who lives in a colony

colony (KAH-luh-nee)—an area that has been settled by people from another country

Declaration of Independence—a document written by Thomas Jefferson in 1776; it declares the United States a free and independent country and says that every U.S. citizen has rights that the government should protect

declare (di-KLAYR)—to make known openly or officially

elect (i-LEKT)—to choose someone as a leader by voting

freedom (FREE-duhm)—the right to live the way you want

government (GUHV-urn-muhnt)—the group of people who make laws, rules, and decisions for a country or state

soldier (SOLE-jur)—a person who is in the military

supplies (suh-PLIZE)—materials needed to do something

surrender (suh-REN-dur)—to give up in battle

tax (TAKS)—money that people or businesses must give to the government to pay for what the government does

train (TRAYN)—to prepare for something by learning and practicing new skills

treaty (TREE-tee)—a written agreement between countries or groups of people. A treaty is signed by the people's leaders.

Read More

Gilpin, Caroline Crosson. *George Washington.* Readers Bios. Washington, D.C.: National Geographic, 2014.

Niver, Heather Moore. *20 Fun Facts About the Declaration of Independence.* Fun Fact File: US History. New York: Gareth Stevens Publishing, 2014.

Raum, Elizabeth. *The Scoop on Clothes, Homes, and Daily Life in Colonial America.* Life in the American Colonies. Mankato, MN: Capstone Press, 2012.

Internet Sites

FactHound offers a safe, fun way to find Internet sites related to this book. All of the sites on FactHound have been researched by our staff.

Here's all you do:

Visit *www.facthound.com*

Type in this code: 9781515724766

Super-cool stuff! Check out projects, games and lots more at **www.capstonekids.com**

Critical Thinking Using the Common Core

1. At the start of the war, what struggles did Washington's army face? (Key Ideas and Details)

2. What reasons did colonists have to be upset with Great Britain? (Integration of Knowledge and Ideas)

Index